Discovering Nature's Hidden Alphabet

DISCOVERING NATURE'S HIDDEN ALPHABET

Krystina Castella and Brian Boyl

Heyday, Berkeley, California

For Sequoia:

Strengthen your roots
Spread your branches
Sing with the breeze
Summon your power
Reach for the sky

Book Design: Rebecca LeGates
Jacket Design: Diane Lee and Rebecca LeGates

Orders, inquiries, and correspondence should be
addressed to:

Heyday
P.O. Box 9145, Berkeley, CA 94709
(510) 549-3564, Fax (510) 549-1889
www.heydaybooks.com

Library of Congress Cataloging-in-Publication Data
Names: Castella, Krystina, author. | Boyl, Brian, author.
Title: Discovering nature's hidden alphabet / Krystina
Castella and Brian
  Boyl.
Description: Berkeley, California : Heyday, [2016] |
Audience: Ages 4-8.
Identifiers: LCCN 2015042679 | ISBN 9781597143592
(hardcover : alk. paper)
Subjects: LCSH: Natural history--Juvenile literature. |
English
  language--Alphabet--Juvenile literature.
Classification: LCC QH48 .C374 2016 | DDC 508--dc23
LC record available at http://lccn.loc.gov/2015042679

Printed in Malaysia by TWP

10 9 8 7 6 5 4 3 2 1

Letter shapes are everywhere in nature—in clouds and trees, in mountains and leaves.

This book is full of hidden letters. Can you find them?

When you think you've found a letter, look again! More than one might be hiding....

letters can hide in
curious places

on paths

Napali Coast Trail (near the wettest place on earth), Kauai, Hawaii
Roots grow in directions that help trees drink as much water as possible. Often roots cross each other on their search for water, making shapes like the letter A.

on the wing

Desolation Wilderness, Lake Tahoe Basin, California
The beautiful patterns on butterfly wings can camouflage them from predators in flowers and leaves. Their bright colors can also be a warning that says, "Don't eat me. I might be toxic!"

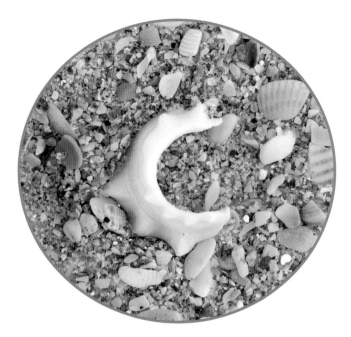

where the sea
leaves its traces

Palm Beach, Florida

A seashell is made as the protective outer layer of a soft creature like a clam or sea snail. After that creature has died and gone, a hermit crab might move in and make the shell its home. Eventually, the ocean waves grind old shells into the sand that makes our beautiful beaches.

in the sky

John Muir Trail, Eastern Sierra Nevada, California

The moon is always round, but sometimes it looks like a D, and other times like a crescent sliver. From earth we only see the moon's sunlit portion, making it appear to change shape as it travels around the earth.

in the trees

Sequoia National Park, California
Can you tell from this charred, black tree
trunk that there was once a fire here?
Natural forest fires are good for the
ecosystem. They thin overgrown forests,
help pinecones disperse their seeds, and
put nutrients into the soil.

in a meadow in spring

Lone Pine, California
The snow on the mountains might make
it look like this photo was taken during
winter, but in fact it is spring and the desert
is bursting with dandelion wildflowers.

in a spiraling twig

Kings Canyon National Park, California
This dry twig was once a living branch that
likely curled while reaching for sunlight.

H

where weathered
pines cling

Inyo National Forest, Cottonwood Lakes, California

Seasons in the mountains are harsh, filled with deep snow in the winter, direct sunrays in the summer, and wind all of the time. Some pine trees thrive and others die, turning into beautiful sculptural letterforms.

on a vast mountain glacier

Rocky Mountain National Park, Colorado
Glaciers are fields of ice that remain in the mountains even in summertime. Some are made of hundreds of years of accumulated ice. If temperatures get warmer over time, glaciers begin to shrink; the dot and base of this "i" were probably once connected!

on bark that is scarred

Black Canyon of the Gunnison National Park, Colorado

The scar on this aspen tree is the tree's natural way of healing itself from damage. Damage like this can be caused by insects burrowing, bears scratching, deers rubbing their antlers, and birds sucking out sap. What do you think happened here?

in old fallen trees

Duck Lake, near Mammoth Lakes, California

Fallen trees create a source of nutrients for wildlife in the forest. They provide a home for insects, which in turn become food for larger animals.

in a broken rock shard

Saddlebag Lake, California
Rocks become smaller over time through their contact with heat, water, ice, and other rocks. This L started out as an enormous shelf of granite, and eventually it will become tiny particles and part of the soil.

M

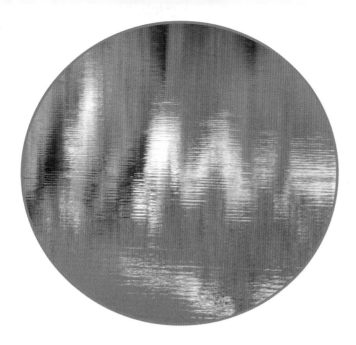

some reflect in a lake

Muir Lake, California
Reflections are light bouncing off of the
surface of the water, showing us our world
upside down. Have you ever noticed that a
W can make a reflected M?

some depend on position

Lang Park, Laguna Beach, California
This N is made from two trees that are
actually twenty feet apart, one in front of
the other. When you stand in the right spot,
the N appears.

some are etched
over time

Los Padres National Forest, California
This rock looks like it was once surrounded by water, with just its top poking out. When the water disappeared, the water's minerals left an O on the rock. Maybe this used to be a creek!

some mark a transition

Descanso Gardens, La Canada, California

Things in nature are often shaped in spheres, circles, and spirals. A spiral starts at one point and circles out from the center, going around and around. This fern *grows* in a spiral, slowly unfurling itself.

look at knots

Long Meadow, Cottonwood Lakes, California
Knots are formed where branches grow.
This Q shows us where a branch once lived
and has since fallen off.

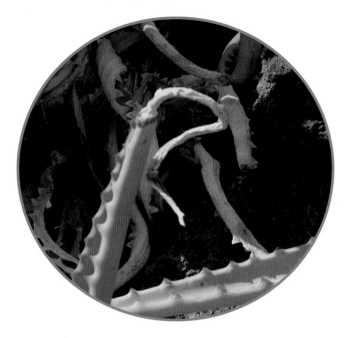

look at tendrils

The Huntington, San Marino, California
Succulents are plants that grow in hot, dry places. They are great at storing water in their fleshy stems. Often their tips dry out, forming curling shapes like this R.

and river meanders

**Tuolumne River, Lyell Canyon,
Yosemite National Park, California**
In a flat valley with soft soil, a river curves
like this naturally. If soil caves in on one
side, the water rushes in and shifts its flow
against the opposite bank. After enough
time, a curve is formed.

among leaves

Kings Canyon National Park, California
In spring and summer these leaves were green with chlorophyll capturing sunlight. In shorter autumn days with less sunlight, trees made less chlorophyll. The leaves lost their green, turned beautiful colors, then fell to the ground. Now in winter they are dry and brown, camouflaging this T-shaped branch.

between mountains

Arches National Park, Utah
Rain and wind caused this soft sandstone
rock mountain to erode over time into a U.

on cliffs full of
grandeur

Yosemite National Park, California
At three thousand feet tall, El Capitan
is the largest standing granite rock in
the world. Geologists think the rock was
most likely formed 100 million years ago.
Today, hundreds of rock climbers scale its
face every year, using its many cracks as
handholds and footholds.

W

look closely at everything

San Marino, California
This flower is often called a "bird of paradise" because it looks a little like a bird. Sunbirds perch on its "beak" while they drink its nectar. The birds' feet get covered in pollen, which they bring with them from flower to flower, fertilizing the flowers and helping to make more of them!

letters abound!

Maui, Hawaii

This garden spider waits outstretched for insects to get entangled in the fine silk threads of its web. The zigzag next to the spider's leg is made of spider silk too. Scientists think spiders make these zigzags either to attract prey, or to show other animals the web is there so they won't run into it.

Y

from your feet to the sky

John Muir Trail, Sierra Nevada, California

Sometimes trees stand for years after they've died, especially in the high mountains where the harsh environment limits their decay—there aren't as many insects here to eat them! Dead trees become useful perches for birds resting, hunting, and nesting.

they are found all around!

Cumberland Island, Georgia

Clouds are made of warm air, dust particles, and tiny water droplets that are so light they float. Different cloud shapes move through the sky with the wind. At sunset, beams of sunlight pierce through the gaps between clouds with magnificent power.

Authors' Note

Discovering the alphabet in nature helps us slow down and appreciate how interesting the world is. Finding letters may seem hard at first, but when we change the way we look, we can see things we've never seen before. Letters can appear when you look closely, and when you look far away. Some are buried deep, and others hidden in plain sight. Letters can even appear right before your eyes: a deer turns his head and his antlers make a perfect V. The sun hits a tree root just right to make a Z.

We found these letters by hiking and exploring in all kinds of places: forests, beaches, deserts, mountains, and parks. Although we love taking pictures of the letters we find, discovering them is the greatest thrill of all.

Play Your Own
Hidden Alphabet Game

The rule: You cannot touch anything in order to create a letter—not with your hand, not even with your pinky toe!

Find a good place to play. You can play anywhere—at home, at school, while taking a walk in your community. But it's especially fun to play this game in places where you're surrounded by nature, like your neighborhood park, the beach, or a forest.

Scan the scene in front of you. Look for the kinds of structures and patterns that make letters: straight lines and curvy lines, crosses and kinks, spirals and squiggles. Look out as far as you can see, and look down at the ground right in front of you. Walk around and look from different angles.

When you start to see a letter shape emerge, the trick is to position yourself so you can see the letter as clearly as possible. Then, show your friends or take a picture! Leave the letter there, untouched, for someone else to discover.

About the Authors

Krystina Castella and Brian Boyl are a husband and wife team of designers, photographers, and avid backpackers who consider nature to be a limitless source of inspiration. Their first book, *Discovering Nature's Alphabet,* inspired a museum exhibit and family workshops. It traveled around the USA for many years, motivating viewers to explore nature and photograph their own alphabets.

Krystina and Brian are both professors at Art Center College of Design in Southern California and enjoy letter hunting with their young son, Sequoia.